Di

WILLIAM LETFORD was born ... ꜱ̶t̶i̶r̶l̶i̶n̶g̶, Scotland. He has received an MLitt from Glasgow University, an Edwin Morgan Travel Bursary from the Arts Trust of Scotland, a New Writers' Award from the Scottish Book Trust, and a Creative Scotland Artists' Bursary which allowed him to spend six months travelling through India.

Also by WILLIAM LETFORD
from Carcanet Press

Bevel (2012)

Dirt

WILLIAM LETFORD

for Abi

CARCANET

First published in Great Britain in 2016 by

CARCANET PRESS Ltd
Alliance House, 30 Cross Street
Manchester M2 7AQ
www.carcanet.co.uk

We welcome your feedback on our books:
info@carcanet.co.uk

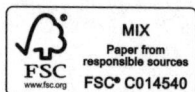

Poems © William Letford, 2016

A CIP catalogue record for this book is available from
the British Library, ISBN 9781784102005

The publisher acknowledges financial assistance
from Arts Council England

Supported using public funding by
ARTS COUNCIL
ENGLAND

Contents

In the back alleys 09

Crocodile 10

In a bamboo shack on the edge of a beach 11

Monuments of the mind 12

Temple 13

'rain' 14

'algae' 15

Gerron 16

Purification 17

Baptism 18

Feedback loop 19

Prayer 20

'the crack' 21

The bevy 22

The performance 24

Gon yursel 25

Wisdom 26

Perfect pitch 27

'OjOs' 28

Curry 29

The north 30

Dream 32

Talknaboot? 33

Marriage 34

Naked 35

Dirt 36

Young Rambo 37

'OjOs' 38

This is it 39

Web 40

'OjOs' 41

'The insistent whistle' 42

Sadness 43

The long dark 44

Delight 45

Let it go 46

The interview 47

The grace 48

The proverbial morning 49

Corporate climate 50

The magic 51

Busy bees 52

A thirst 53

Wake 54

Any way you can 55

Tuesday blues 56

You 57

Circles 58

The grain 59

Every line is imaginary 60

A garden 61

'A series of decisions' 62

Acknowledgements 64

Temples and monuments reach for
transcendence, beauty lies in the
carcass of an insect, cities within cities,
take your eyes from the heavens,
look long and deep.

In the back alleys

Passing midnight in Pushkar I was tracked by a pack of wild dogs, felt real fear when four of them started dartin forward snappin and growlin. I picked up a stick and told myself I would go out swingin. I can lie to myself that way. A local squatting quiet beside a pile of bricks stood up and chased them away, flicked his arms and kicked his legs. The dogs knew the dance. A dance born in streets where hunger growls and hope is majestic, as absent and present as a god.

Crocodile

The low-lying tables were lit by lamps that dropped
from the branches of a banyan tree. Customers ate
beneath patches of light. Focused. Intent. As agreed
the waiter led me past the tables to a clearing, and a
long metallic storage tank. He drew back the latch.
Darkness, and the gentle slap of water. It was there.
Old, and patient. Patient enough to survive the blotting
of the sun. Patient enough to see the passing of the
dinosaurs. Perhaps patient enough for that prison.
Stood still beside the dark I felt the pull of another
language. I could've lowered my hand into the tank.
I wanted to feel its bite. I wanted to hear its music.

In a bamboo shack on the edge of a beach

He read her 'The Moor' by Russell Banks.
It wasn't the story, although the story is good,
and it wasn't the way he read it. The Scottish
accent couldn't quite grasp the Americanisms.
The sures and yeahs became parodies that
brought humour to beauty that didn't need it.
It was the fact that she lay with her head
on his chest and he felt the rumble of his own
voice and a vibration of words gone before.
The story he read ends full of snow, and they
lay very still, but what to do? How long could
they remain there? So he traced patterns on
her skin with his fingers. And the patterns
became circles and the circles became words
and these actions have a tendency to progress.
He lifted her T-shirt over her shoulders and
we know the rest. There are all types of bodies.
If you're lucky you'll find someone whose skin
is a canvas for the story of your life.
Write well. Take care of the heartbeat behind it.

Monuments of the mind

Three men sit at the kitchen table. My grandfather
smokes Golden Virginia. Making a roll-up
has become his ritual. His fingers help him think.
So that's what he does. He teases tobacco from his tin.
My father smokes Silk Cut and has a certain way
of holding a cigarette. Trapping it at the base
of his first two fingers and lifting it to his mouth
so his hand covers the lower half of his face. I don't smoke
but there is a bowl of soup in front of me. Both men
like to see me eat. The room has been stained
by two lifetimes of tobacco smoke, and doesn't
physically exist. But it's where I come for advice. In fact
both men no longer exist, but their voices are as familiar
as my own failings. I slam my spoon onto the table.
Well if that's the way it is then that's the way it is.
'That's the way it is,' says my grandfather.
My father nods his head. He says, 'That is the way it is.'

Temple

The harmony of genders altered his perception of movement. He saw every gesture as a dance. She would take his hands and hold them tight and say, I love the way you see, but I'm trapped. He'd say, You're fusion. The surgery, when it came, proved him wrong. Her post-op pussy was architecture like they couldn't believe. He was brought low before a building constructed to allow his lover out. Gone were bricks and steel and cement. This was flesh.

r r r r r r r r
a a a a a a a a
i i i i i i i i
n n n n n n n n
r r r r r r r r
a a a a a a a a
i i i i i i i i
n n n n n n n n
r r r r r r r r
a a a a a a a a
i i i i i i i i
n n n n n n n n
r r r r r r r r
a a a a a a a a
i i i i i i i i
n n n n n n n n
r r r r r r r r
a a a a a a a a
i i i i i i i i
n n n n n n n n
r r r r r r r r
a a a a a a a a
i i i i i i i i
n n n n n n n n
r r r r r r r r
a a a a a a a a
i i i i i i i i
n n n n n n n n
r r r r r r r r
a a a a a a a a
i i i i i i i i
n n n n n n n n
r r r r r r r r
a a a a a a a a

algae can make rain in Kerala
fall yellow, green, red, or black
rip open the word rain
and you'll find that beaded curtain

Gerron

eeny meeny macca racca ee aye doaminacca sugar
ally lolly pop an tig a say yur het al hae a wee
laugh al jist say aye wae the inky pinky oom pie pie
skeedly weedly wadly wee rigadigadoo an away yi go

Purification

crack open the eyes make fists with feet hangover check negative
stand up totter crease face call it a smile blink wade knee deep
toward coffee percolate wait for first smack of caffeine try again
lift corners of mouth crease face hawk spit roll and lick donder
towards window smoke feel first movement teeter towards ablution

Baptism

He couldn't drop yesterday and he couldn't stop tomorrow
so he listened to the flow and realised that time didn't tick,
it beat like a heart, at the mercy of mood and movement.
Seconds splashed around him. He danced until he drowned.

Feedback loop

she made a sound
and he changed his
rhythm and she made
a sound and he changed
his rhythm and this went
on and on until one gasp
ran into the next and he
couldn't thrust any faster
and she couldn't scream
any louder and thermo–
dynamics reversed and
sweat and skin slapped
like a biological whip
until grunt gasp sigh
thrust they became the
locomotive of creation

Prayer

Da, if thurs a heaven it's here, runnin parallel wae
hell. Alleyways crisscrossin between each street,
closes that aren't quite one or the other. But that
doesn't bother me. Like yi said. I play it as straight
as I can. It's no always easy. Sometimes a fuck up.
Sometimes people fuck me up. I try to forgive them.
I try to forgive myself. I hold on to the love yi gave me.
I try to be vulnerable, so I can let that love in. I look
for beauty in small things. Let the night sky make me
feel small. I don't always know what to believe in,
but it's the unknown that makes life an adventure.
I realise the sacrifice yi made for me, and I miss yi.
But I knew yi. That's somethin to be thankful for.

the crack of a bone the moon and the tide that
brings its song forests of cellos gardens of violins
the silent flap of a worm in mud the groan of bamboo
the sound of frost every orgasm in every bedroom back
room and public toilet the sound of light as it hits the
mouth of a cave skin is a symphony every mirror is
a sheet of music reflection is reverb countless re
reflection is reverb re countless collaborations
atoms that are perfectly pitched a trickle of
water is like a million musicians leaving
their seats and the beat of every heart
everywhere the melody of saliva
the course ground blues of dry
dirt the funk of everything
that lives in it a comet
the sight of it beads
a drop of reverb
you and her
and him
and
me
i

The bevy

a hid met this lassie
she liked the bevy
a like drink masel
bit this lassie liked the bevy
normally a kin keep it in check
play fitbaw n that
go oan benders
bit go a week or two withoot
regain the healthy glow
bit a hid met this lassie
an a goat a red rash beneath ma eyes
fae the bevy
drinkin too much eh it
bit a wiz enjoyin masel
cause we wid huv these brilliant arguments
proabin each other's psyche
searchin fur soft spots
seein wit damage we could dae
bit hodin back
bein cliver
niver punchin the core
cause that wiy
we could cover the soft spots wae affection
that made us feel like
we needed each other
that made us feel like
we could destroy each other
cause fawin in love wae this lassie

wiz like turnin yur chist tae
the universe
an screamin hit me
bit it didnae last
cause time passed
an we realised
we couldnae hurt each other
so am back playin fitbaw n that
gon oan benders like
bit keepin it in check

The performance

I know a man whose burden is a beautiful
brown cello. He carries the instrument in a
cumbersome white case. The case is dented
and scratched, and has seen sunsets from
Santiago to Berlin. The man who carries
the case frowns at every hill. He grumbles
as he shoulders his way through busy streets.
He secretly envies the flautists. But the case
carrier and the musician are not the same.
They are separate in one body. One translates
the great composers through memories of
childhood. The other drinks whisky and spits
phlegm into his sink. They both remember
a visiting cellist that asked their class to raise
a hand. The hand was measured. The musician
says, it was to test the strength of his fingers.
The case carrier will tell you that the cellist
never looked him in the eye.

Gon yursel

am lookin it um thinkin
don't know wit yur sayin

he says, annaromamoof

wit?

annaromamoof

geez it slowly

he says, annar – oma – moof

nay lip movement except fur
a twitch between oma n moof

Wisdom

The boy has asthma. His wheeze is somewhere
between a moan and a whistle, and there is a
pause before each intake, as if it's necessary to
concentrate, to think, breathe. The mother talks,
asking for tickets, and popcorn, and cola.
She grips his shoulder and curls the hair on the
crown of his head. All the while the boy
is watching, and his eyes are electric. They are
wonderful. Big enough so that, if he wanted to,
he could tip his head back and pour the world in.

Perfect pitch

It took fifty years of continual play
for the strings on his violin to alter
his vocal chords. People were suddenly
pulled in his wake. Rather than react
to his words they were transfixed.
His conversation washed over the
public like music. Every friend became
the member of an audience. Dinner
parties became concerts without
applause. He lived the rest of his life
lonely, a prisoner of his perfect pitch.

OjOs

Curry

No laughter, only the moan of a wretch in the dark;
this is war, and the brain is a bystander. He passes
time by imagining each convulsion is a prayer. Odin
is named. Romulus has been summoned. Sixteen
hours later religion gives way to scale. He stares
into wormholes and white cisterns, sees black holes
expelling galaxies. Listens to the chatter of bacteria
and an increasing population.

The north

The boy was born in the dirt, on the flat of the carse;
premature and caked in mud, soil and blood on his skin.

No ordinary child they said, eyes as green as leaves,
roots that shook at the scream, then the rain.

As a man he stood apart, strong as the silence of trees,
braw as a forest stream, steady as the coming dark.

Hard were the veins that ran to his heart, love would
make them bloom though, and burst the coming dark.

The girl was born on the crag, when the light was fierce;
premature and washed in sun, her birth was like a song.

No ordinary child they said, sky in her eyes,
blue as you'll ever get, gaze like a day without an end.

A women that walked alone, braw as the last flower,
clever as heartfelt laughter, steady as waves on a shore.

Alone she walked though, like sunshine through glass,
until she met the coming dark, until the seed met the spark.

They found each other in a city, far from the crag and the dirt
where roadways ran like arteries, and the city beat like a heart.

Tail lights and headlights rushed, in a flow as thick as blood;
banks and parliaments throbbed, and the city beat like a heart.

No ordinary love they said, as flowers grew on kerbs, as vines crept along pavements, in the city that beat like a heart.

Roadways ran like arteries, flowing as thick as blood, the wind that came from the north blew dark and sky and sun and dirt.

And the city beat like a heart, and the city beat like a heart, vines cracked the pavements, and the city beat like a heart.

Dream

For years I could stand by my window and watch clouds climb
over the Ochil Hills, sunshine burst against rooftops, kitchens
blink into life when most of Stirling was dreaming. Then the attic
window in Winchester. One tree filling the glass. The seasons
leaf by leaf. Every window is a singular experience. No two
offer the same view. Mirrors are windows reversed. The seasons
turn but they turn inside us. Lights blink into life. We dream.

Talknaboot?

annaromamoof

neerda

so wit eh yi talknaboot

am sayin annaromamoof

aye well neerda

Marriage

I could take this opportunity
to wish you love and happiness
but you've already got that.
No, my wish for you
is the incidental, the ordinary,
to know someone
by the way their fork moves across a plate,
to see the majesty in someone's back, sleeping.
My wish for you
is twenty thousand mornings
climbing out of bed together.
My wish for you
is twenty thousand sunsets
that you can't see
because the curtains are closed and
you're sitting in a room talking about
nothing in particular.

Let the special occasions
take care of themselves,
learn to recognise
the wonder in the everyday.

My wish for you is a life lived together
filled with breakfasts, suppers, spoons and pillows.

Naked

If i could give someone
a gift
it would be the ability
to look through time
and see you
as I see you now,
naked
and full of adventure.
The gift
is impossible
but know this,
I see you.

Dirt

I want the dust beneath the fridge to hold the DNA
of generations. I want to lift the delicate carcass
of an insect from the carpet. I want to sit by the window
and watch water in the gutter and when I pull back the
sheets I want them dirty. I want the dirt on my hands.
I want it wet because there's rain and I've trucked
through mud to get here. I want saliva and spit and I
want that part of your mind. To celebrate it. To act it out.
There's dignity there. Lay yourself open. We'll both
blossom. If you want me to call you a whore, I'll do it.
Stand in the muck with me. Live amongst the flowers.

Young Rambo

We were working high up on a hillside
with a view over the valley, clouds moving
slow, no wind, sunshine slanting through
in massive shafts, whole towns lit up,
and he was breaking slates, hammering
too hard, aiming beyond the nails, striking
his imagination, or his memory. I decided
I could help. I waited for lunch and sat
facing him using my toolbox as a seat.
Johnny, I said, do you know about the goddess
of fortune? He lifted his eyes and replied
by chewing his corned beef. There was a
flatness in his stare, like there was nothing
else around and he could see me.
I said, She carries a rudder in one hand
and flowers in the other, wherever she is
flowers are falling from the sky, but she's
blind, and as soon as she turns the rudder...
I left the sentence open. He dropped his crust
on the shale and said, Young Rambo, give
yourself time, you'll realise the rudder's broken
and she's throwing shite, we can eat it or drown.
He got up, walked away, and seemed happier
for the rest of the day. It's questionable whether
it was my wisdom that improved his mood.

OjOs

This is it

Skint, baw ragged, poackets ful eh ma
fingers, cannae afford tae burn toast an
it's November, Christmas is close. Av been
away bit noo am back an ivery coarner
is a different colour cause am hame an
memories ur painted wae mischief. Am
ootside Gregs eatin a macaroni pie an a
busker picks up eez guitar an plugs in eez
amplifier. The sound fae the strings is
like frost. Eez young an the dreams thit
wur boarn in eez bedroom wake me up.
Am watchin people passin an they know
thit eez good bit they don't want tae look.
They turn thur heeds an tilt thur ears
an jog on. If a hud a spare pound
a wid throw it bit a don't so a jist listen.
I'd like tae tell um thit this is it, this is
where the hammer hits the stane an sparks
ur made, standin oan a coarner in yur hame
toon, an audience eh one radge eatin a
macaroni pie, bit singin, wee man, yur singin.

Web

there may be a very big spider in the barn
said the wise old owl

OjOs OjOs OjOs OjOs OjOs OjOs OjOs OjOs OjOs OjOs
OjOs OjOs OjOs OjOs OjOs OjOs OjOs OjOs OjOs OjOs
OjOs OjOs OjOs OjOs OjOs OjOs OjOs OjOs OjOs OjOs
OjOs OjOs OjOs OjOs OjOs OjOs OjOs OjOs OjOs OjOs
OjOs OjOs OjOs OjOs OjOs OjOs OjOs OjOs OjOs OjOs
OjOs OjOs OjOs OjOs OjOs OjOs OjOs OjOs OjOs OjOs
OjOs OjOs OjOs OjOs OjOs OjOs OjOs OjOs OjOs OjOs
OjOs OjOs OjOs OjOs OjOs OjOs OjOs OjOs OjOs OjOs
OjOs OjOs OjOs OjOs OjOs OjOs OjOs OjOs OjOs OjOs
OjOs OjOs OjOs OjOs OjOs OjOs OjOs OjOs OjOs OjOs
OjOs OjOs OjOs OjOs OjOs OjOs OjOs OjOs OjOs OjOs
OjOs OjOs OjOs OjOs OjOs OjOs OjOs OjOs OjOs OjOs
OjOs OjOs OjOs OjOs OjOs OjOs OjOs OjOs OjOs OjOs
OjOs OjOs OjOs OjOs OjOs OjOs OjOs OjOs OjOs OjOs
OjOs OjOs OjOs OjOs OjOs OjOs OjOs OjOs OjOs OjOs
OjOs OjOs OjOs OjOs OjOs OjOs OjOs OjOs OjOs OjOs
OjOs OjOs OjOs OjOs OjOs OjOs OjOs OjOs OjOs OjOs
OjOs OjOs OjOs OjOs OjOs OjOs OjOs OjOs OjOs OjOs
OjOs OjOs OjOs OjOs OjOs OjOs OjOs OjOs OjOs OjOs
OjOs OjOs OjOs OjOs OjOs OjOs OjOs OjOs OjOs OjOs
OjOs OjOs OjOs OjOs OjOs OjOs OjOs OjOs OjOs OjOs
OjOs OjOs OjOs OjOs OjOs OjOs OjOs OjOs OjOs OjOs
OjOs OjOs OjOs OjOs OjOs OjOs OjOs OjOs OjOs OjOs
OjOs OjOs OjOs OjOs OjOs OjOs OjOs OjOs OjOs OjOs
OjOs OjOs OjOs OjOs OjOs OjOs OjOs OjOs OjOs OjOs
OjOs OjOs OjOs OjOs OjOs OjOs OjOs OjOs OjOs OjOs
OjOs OjOs OjOs OjOs OjOs OjOs OjOs OjOs OjOs OjOs
OjOs OjOs OjOs OjOs OjOs OjOs OjOs OjOs OjOs OjOs
OjOs OjOs OjOs OjOs OjOs OjOs OjOs OjOs OjOs OjOs
OjOs OjOs OjOs OjOs OjOs OjOs OjOs OjOs OjOs OjOs
OjOs OjOs OjOs OjOs OjOs OjOs OjOs OjOs OjOs OjOs
OjOs OjOs OjOs OjOs OjOs OjOs OjOs OjOs OjOs OjOs
OjOs OjOs OjOs OjOs OjOs OjOs OjOs OjOs OjOs OjOs
OjOs OjOs OjOs OjOs OjOs OjOs OjOs OjOs OjOs OjOs

The insistent whistle of the train overhead pierced the night sky like a high rise and the unsteady rhythm of a stolen drum gave form to the arches on the underside of a bridge as a fire threw faltering light on the faces of the huddled and cold whose eyes were white like the stars and piercing like whistles. The huddled and cold passed whispers to each other like dreams in the dirt until their minds became as restless as skyscrapers.

Sadness

The sadness inside him went deep. The vast distance between every nucleus and every electron in his body was a well that could never be filled. Beauty entered and was lost. Wonder entered and was lost. People were drawn to him because they fell, and the feeling of falling was like flying. His eyes were pathways to forever, and everyone who loved him was lost.
His death was a doorway being closed and the world became smaller for it.

The long dark

His tongue has flattened until the tip can lick like a razor
and lash back and forth striking blind, vindictive, careless.
She has the cutlery eyes that can telekinetically unthread
the open nerve of every sentence and the battle has raged
from room to room. The bed a coffin, the bathroom
a locked cell. In the kitchen their cute blue kettle chokes
on every boil. The night has been long and the sunrise is
like black bleeding but the sun does rise. And with it comes
understanding. Panting, breathless, brain-tired. Exultation.
The necessary exorcism. The dance of dark and day.

Delight

I keep my red stiletto heels in the freezer – cooling, frosting, they keep me sane. And after work, I kick off my steel toe-capped boots, roll up my jeans to the knee, and lift those red stilettos from that middle drawer. Smoke tumbles to the kitchen floor, and the cold crack of the leather makes the colour all the brighter. How magical to become so tall in my own home, to dance while standing still, to travel without moving.

Let it go

My sphincter pouts like a smoker's lips.
I panic for a time. Big wide eyes.
Tiptoes. Then all is lost, and I lumber
toward the hostel, like a monkey in the
jungle of traffic, stinking, wild and free.

The interview

A middle-management centaur, half man
half desk, imbued with authority power,
collars for shoulders, buttons for nipples.
Lips like a paper clip. 'So,' he says, in a flat,
wooden tone, 'tell me your positive attributes.'
I only have one so I tell him the truth.
I say, 'I'm greedy. Gluttony is my positive
attribute. I want everything, and I don't mean
the money you're offering. Capital is desire
for the deluded. I want loneliness, because
loneliness is beautiful. I want love because
love is pain, and pain is essential. I want
fear. Fear is fact. I want all the lust life can
muster. Lust is the push. My mother pushed.
Normal doesn't exist so give me madness.
I want it all. The whole lot. No holding back.'

The grace

We met drinking sweet masala chai in a dirty cafe.
His wife had bought him a ticket to travel the world
for his seventy-fifth birthday. His possessions were
stripped to the essential. He carried a backpack and
a suntan. With ease of movement came an easy grace.
He walked like a poem stepping off a page.

The proverbial morning

The alarm had been silenced and their
eyes weren't fully open and their faces
were swollen from sleep.

She said, Ugh, I don't want to go to work.

He said, You can do anything you want, the world is yours.

She said, Can I become a panda?

He said, Course you can, it would take some deep
meditation and a lot of genetics but it's possible.
He thought for a moment, You would be one skinny-ass
panda though.

She said, I'd look like a cat, or a skunk. People would
look at me and say, You're not an endangered panda,
you're a skunk. Then *bang bang*, they'd shoot me.
Anyway, she said, I've got to go to work.

Corporate climate

He was talking through an imagined version of himself, as if the wind he created was blowing up his own ass.

The magic

On a cold day steam rises from the loch.
It's the thermocline. Surface water cools
then sinks, replaced by warm water one
hundred feet below. Today is a cold day
and a family has gathered by the bank
to see the monster, I think, but the mist
is a shield, and the family seems to be stood
by a cloud. One young girl is skimming
stones that skip the water and cut the mist.
An elderly man is leaning on a cane,
standing apart. I approach. His eyes are
more blue than sky. The kind of blue you
can't reach. I try anyway. Are you a believer?
I ask. He frowns. Then he smiles and
history appears in the lines of his face.
He nods at the loch and says, That water
is deeper than we can fathom. It's our
imagination that's moving beneath. He lifts
his cane and points at the girl. Possibility
is all that's important.

Busy bees

Sometimes they struggled to pay the bills. They were never hungry but they couldn't get ahead and they lived in a very small flat. Luckily, most of the things that made them happy happened inside their own heads. There seemed to be room to grow in there so obviously, in a way, everything was okay. But many minds were beginning to grow. Ideas were carried from one living room to the next. Conversations unfolded.

A *thirst*

I didn't expect to find a book on cutting-edge
theoretical physics tucked behind the cushion
on the elegant armchair. She laughed and
said she didn't fully understand it, that being
surprised was enough. Said she was turning
the pages more slowly these days, savouring
each word. And that she was confident, by the
end, she would be left with a sense of wonder.

Wake

Gerron big man yur a cracker, geez a cuddle,
dinnae be feart oor herts ur big enough no
eh lit oor biceps get in the wiy. Wur warriors.
Remember yur mam? So dae a, that's wit am
talkin aboot, see that belly button, stick yur
finger in it. Nae tears in yur pint that's wit
yur puhlla's fur. Mon, al walk yi up the road.

Any way you can

On Friday I visit my seventy-seven-year-old
granny. She's smoking a joint. It's not a surprise.
My mother introduced it to her a couple of years
back, right after my grandfather died. When the
tea and biscuits are finally finished she shows me
a speech she recited in the eighties, to the miners,
she shows me photographs of her and Arthur
Scargill. It's then that I realise she doesn't inhale.
For her it's more like a gesture. Well then god
love you granny. Fuck them all, any way you can.

Tuesday blues

The room is an engine of rising elbows. Every drink
is a slap in the face. Empty glass follows empty glass
until the guitar hits a nerve and the snare drum opens
a door. We rise, slow, awful, rotten with wonder, a grind
of bones delicious with decrepitude. The dance floor
becomes language as the big barman shifts his muscle
like mud sliding from a mountain. He plucks one more
bottle from the back shelf and blows dust at the flies.

You

are a veritable popinjay
who incessantly exacerbates
my general feeling of malcontent

!?

annaromamoof

Circles

I'm sure I've heard that lives move
like circles. Acquaintances being
overlapping lines, like sketching an
endless series of Olympic symbols.
So if two lines meet, a friendship
begins. The next time they meet
that friendship will end. Taking this
as truth, I'm asking what about us?
Your line, though gone, begins to
trace once again those semi-sincere
professions of love. Perhaps two arcs
can shape a moon, and to a world of
lines, add some colour. This gives me
hope, although never too soon, that I
may be round again, dancing in splendour.

The grain

She would sit by the corner of King Street with a blanket across her lap. Never talking, always watching. She was beautiful. Her skin was as rutted as the bark of a tree. The bark of a tree that could shift and flow. It was like I could trace every line on her face back to its source, back to its seed. Her ageing body had fallen against the sum of her thoughts. And I could see the grain of her spirit.

Every line is imaginary

A jumble of bodies bobbing and shifting.
There is sweat, and rhythm, and pain.
One turn from the end.
He is last.
I wish he already knew
that finishing lines don't really exist,
that the trick is not stopping.
But he is twelve years old,
full of summer
and, would you believe it, coming up fast.

A garden

Mr and Mrs Clarke owned the house.
An elderly couple, well travelled with
a sharp sense of humour and lots of
laughter lines. Mr Clarke had gone
blind late in his life and as he listened
to me talk through the job, he smiled.
I wasn't trying to be funny but they were
a lovely couple and I took his good
mood as a compliment. I'd taken a break
about midday and was looking down
from the roof into their garden. Mrs Clarke
was trying to lift a growbag into a
wheelbarrow. She couldn't cope and she
called for her husband. Mr Clarke appeared
at the back door and brushed his body
against plants and flowers to feel his
way toward the greenhouse. He lifted
the bag then hefted the handles of the
wheelbarrow. He was strong for an
old man. He waited. Mrs Clarke took his
elbow and led him out of the greenhouse,
talking to him all the way. They moved
with confidence. The wheelbarrow trundled
in front. Can't recall if the job was in
Kippen or Balquidder but I remember how
beautiful their garden was. Full of colour.

A series of decisions have been made
the consequences of which will have
repercussions of great beauty

Acknowledgements

Some of these poems first appeared in *This Room is Waiting*, *Cordite Poetry Review*, and *Neu Reekie: #UntitledOne*. The poem 'Monuments of the mind' was written as a commission for the Enlighten Edinburgh Project. The poem 'Every line is imaginary' was written as a commission for The Scottish Poetry Library to celebrate the close of The Written World Project. 'The performance' was written as a commission for the Theatre Royal. 'The grain' was written as a commission for the Scottish Book Trust. 'Marriage' was written at the request of my cousin, Sheena, for her wedding.

Special thanks are due to Creative Scotland for the award of an Artists' Bursary, which allowed me to travel through India for six months. The bursary gave me more than time to write, and experiences that informed this collection – India is where I met my wife.